"Coo-coo-coo," said the dove.
"One and one make two, my love."

"Caw-caw-caw," cried the crow.
"Two and two make four, you know."

"Twee-twee-twee,"
came from a tree.
"One and one and one make three,
meaning you and you and me,"
chirped some sparrows in a tree.

"Four and four, we think, make eight," squawked some brown birds on a gate.

"Well, six and four, I know, make ten. Just count my chicks," clucked the hen.

"Five and four add up to nine," sang the magpies on the line.